TAMESIDE LIBRARIES
3 8016 01395 4377

D0518833

www.Tameside.gov.uk
HYDE LIBRARY

WITHDRAWN FROM
TAMESIDE LIBRARIES

I love YOGA

LONDON, NEW YORK, MUNICH,
MELBOURNE, AND DELHI

Editor Elizabeth Hester
Assistant Managing Art Director Michelle Baxter
Design Assistant Jessica Lasher
Publishing Director Beth Sutinis
Art Director Dirk Kaufman
Creative Director Tina Vaughan
Production Ivor Parker
DTP Milos Orlovic

Photographer Angela Coppola

First published in Great Britain in 2006 by Dorling Kindersley Limited,
80 Strand, London WC2R 0RL

06 07 08 09 10 9 8 7 6 5 4 3 2 1

Copyright © 2006 Dorling Kindersley Limited

All images © Dorling Kindersley Limited
All photographs in this book were taken by Angela Coppola except:
Dog (Steve Shott © Dorling Kindersley Limited) and
Cat (© Dorling Kindersley Limited), both on page 11.
For more information see: www.dkimages.com

All rights reserved. No part of this publication may be reproduced,
stored in a retrieval system, or transmitted in any form or by any means,
electronic, mechanical, photocopying, recording, or otherwise,
without the prior written permission of the copyright owner.

ISBN-13: 978-1-40531-435-0
ISBN-10: 1-4053-1435-4

Reproduced by Colourscan, Singapore
Printed and bound in China by L.Rex

Discover more at
www.dk.com

I love YOGA

Written by Mary Kaye Chryssicas
Photography by Angela Coppola

Contents

TAMESIDE M.B.C.
LIBRARIES

01395437	
Bertrams	30.03.06
J613.7046	£7.99

Introduction

Yoga teaches us how to pay attention to our bodies and use our own breath to put our minds at peace. Practising yoga can help you face stressful situations and keep your body strong. It's fun to learn how many wonderful ways your body can move!

Arriving at Class

The students are arriving at the yoga studio. Each child brings a yoga mat and wears comfortable clothes that make it easy to move and stretch. Some of the students, like Caroline and Anna, have been taking yoga for a few years. Grant is just beginning to learn yoga, but Tara and the other students help him feel comfortable. The class always welcomes new students. That's part of what yoga is all about!

Caroline and Anna have become good friends through yoga class.

Getting ready

Tara helps Grant get ready for class. Grant wears comfortable shorts and a vest so he can move around easily. Tara wears soft cotton yoga pants and a fitted top. They take off jackets, jewellery and shoes before class begins.

What to bring

Everything each student needs for class fits into this mat bag. The mat is the most important piece of yoga equipment. Its surface is a little sticky, so it helps keep hands and feet in place during poses. It's also wise to bring a bottle of water to drink during class.

Long hair should be pulled away from the face so it won't be distracting during class.

“I made some of my best friends at yoga.”

Caroline

Yoga props

The teacher provides yoga props to make difficult poses easier, or to help students get used to new positions. Blocks can help with balance. Straps can be useful for stretching poses. A blanket can pad your knees or your seat to make you feel more comfortable. And eye pillows are a relaxing reward at the end of class.

Blocks and blankets

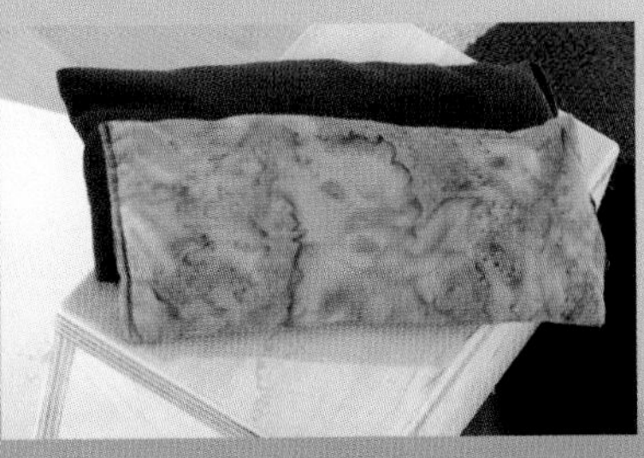

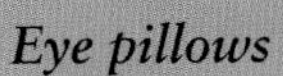

Eye pillows

Strap

What is Yoga?

Yoga was first practised thousands of years ago as a way to exercise and to calm the mind, or meditate. Yoga is built around a series of poses. In the beginning, yoga focused mainly on seated poses for meditation. Then people who practised yoga, called yogis (yoh-gees), added more active poses. Today, people all over the word do yoga to help keep their bodies and minds healthy.

Mary Kaye is an experienced yogi who has studied the best ways to teach poses. She shows how to do each pose during class, and then checks to make sure each student is on the right track.

Sun Salutations

Sun Salutations are a way for people to start their day or begin a class with energy. Mary Kaye demonstrates this exercise, which is a sequence of poses linked together. Over time, the class will learn to use the breath to move fluidly between poses in Sun Salutations and other sequences.

Yoga is a way of life

The patience and calm you learn during yoga helps you accept challenges in life. Mary Kaye encourages the class to remember yoga during stressful times, like before a big football game or spelling test, to help them relax.

Yoga names

The names of yoga poses describe the animal or object they imitate. There are poses called Gorilla, Cobra, Mountain and Tree. Some poses look a lot like their names. Some take a little more imagination. Each pose also has a name in Sanskrit, an ancient language from India, where yoga was born.

Cat pose

Have you ever seen a cat arch his back? Mary Kaye shows how Cat pose imitates this stretch. The body begins on all fours, and the back is rounded like a cat.

Downward Dog pose

If you have a dog, you've probably seen him do yoga! This pose is called Downward Dog. In Sanskrit it's called Adho Mukha Svanasana *(ahd-oh moo-ka svan-ah-sah-nah).*

Miles tries a Lion's Breath. He breathes in and out with an open mouth and says "ha!"

Warming Up

First, everyone finds a space on the floor to unroll their yoga mats. When everyone is ready to begin, Mary Kaye invites the class to sit with her on the floor. She explains that the most important part of yoga is the breath. Paying attention to the breath can help yogis stay strong in poses and keep the mind at peace. Class begins with some simple breathing exercises.

The breath

Mary Kaye asks the students to inhale, or breathe in, filling their bellies with air. Then they exhale, or breathe out, as if fogging up a window. The students then try this breathing exercise with their mouths closed. This is called Ujjayi (oo-jiy) breathing.

Lotus pose

Easy pose is a simpler version of Lotus.

Caroline settles into Lotus pose by folding each foot against the opposite hip. The hands rest on the knees.

Lotus Lift

Caroline does Lotus Lift by pressing her palms to the floor and lifting her body up.

Lotus Stretch

A gentle stretch in Lotus helps Caroline warm up for class. She rests one hand on the floor while the other reaches overhead.

Seated forward bend

This pose stretches the leg muscles and loosens the body. Don't worry if you can't reach your feet – just try to keep your legs and back straight.

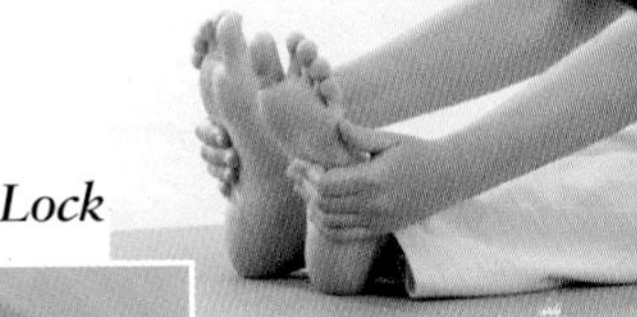

Miles uses a strap to help him do this stretch.

Yoga Toe Lock

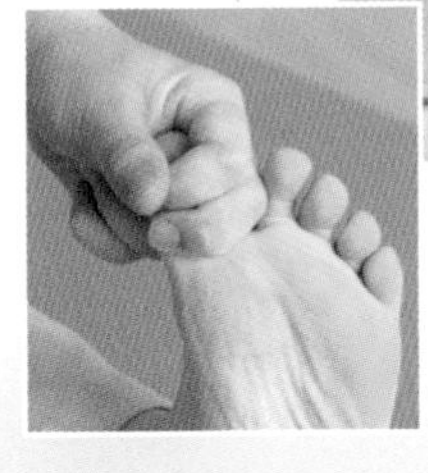

Sit on your mat with legs extended. Slowly walk the fingers down the legs and towards the toes. Try holding a toe in Yoga Toe Lock for a deeper stretch.

Foot Stretch

Mary Kaye calls this stretch 'waterskiing'. Sit on your heels with your knees in front. Keep the feet flat. Raise your arms to take hold of the ski rope. Try to touch the water!

This is the counterpose for Foot Stretch. Counterpose means opposite pose. A pose and its counterpose are often done one after the other to keep the body balanced.

Grant presses his palms together in Prayer position.

Waking Up the Body

It's time to wake up the body with some basic poses. The children learn to use their breath as they move in and out of poses. Mary Kaye reminds everyone that basic poses like these will come up again and again in class, so it's important for each student to pay close attention to the breath and the movement of the body.

Miles stands with the quiet strength of a mountain in Mountain pose. The palms rest in Prayer position in front of the heart, and the legs and back are straight.

From Mountain pose, Miles jumps up high, spreading his arms and legs wide. He exhales a loud Lion's Breath: Haaa! The volcano erupts!

Downward Dog

This is a basic pose that can lead to lots of other poses. In Downward Dog, the arms and legs are straight, and the chest presses down toward the mat. Try to push your feet and hands flat against the mat.

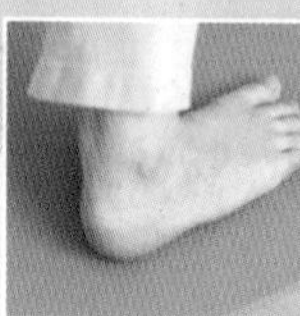

In Downward Dog, feet are flat and slightly pigeon-toed.

Spread your fingers like a starfish.

Dolphin

From Downward Dog, Caroline drops her elbows to the mat into Dolphin pose.

Upward Dog

Upward Dog is the counterpose of Downward Dog. In Upward Dog, the head is held high and straight and the arms are strong. Anna can lift her thighs off the ground in this pose. It's also OK to keep them on the mat while you're learning.

Plank

Plank pose makes your body strong and lengthens the spine. Look at a spot between your hands as you try to keep your body in a straight line. But don't worry about doing the pose 'perfectly' – there is no perfect pose.

"Plank pose makes my whole body feel alive!"
Anna

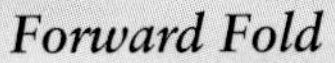

Forward Fold

After all these energetic poses, Tara clasps her hands together and folds over to stretch her shoulders and rest. Mary Kaye says the head should feel heavy like a watermelon hanging from a vine.

Lightning Bolt

Lightning Bolt is an active pose that energizes the body. The fingertips reach to the sky like lightning. Tara keeps her knees and feet together and tries to feel energy reaching out.

Peacock Feather

Caroline lifts her right foot to the sky. The palms and heel press into the mat. Mary Kaye helps keep her hips parallel to the mat.

Lift Up Your Heart

These poses are designed to help lift the heart and open the chest. Caroline likes the way this feels – like the mind is opening to new ideas as the body learns to stretch into a more open position. These exercises promote flexibility and coordination and help you feel good about yourself.

Cobra pose

Grant presses up into Cobra pose. Cobra keeps the spine as flexible as a snake. Grant tries to lift his ears away from his shoulders and hold his chest up.

Stick out your tongue like a cobra!

Fish pose

Anna tilts her head back in Fish pose. She rests on her elbows and arches her chest. Mary Kaye says that in this pose your chest should feel like it's smiling!

Camel pose

This pose looks like the hump of a camel's back. The girls begin this pose in a kneeling position. Then they press the hips forwards as they arch their backs. The hands reach down to take hold of the heels. Mary Kaye reminds them to drop their heads back, close their eyes and breathe.

One-arm Camel

Anna reaches one arm to the sky in another version of Camel. In yoga, one pose can have lots of forms. Your teacher can help you find the one that feels best for you.

"When I drop back in Camel, I can feel my heart beat."
Christine

Child's pose

Child's Pose is a restful pose that feels good after Camel – or any time you feel tired in class.

Hip Openers

Hip-opening poses like Dancer's Pose encourage stability, balance and the ability to focus. They open the hips and leave you feeling energized. Hold each hip-opening pose for several breaths and try to concentrate so you can hold the pose longer.

Hip stretches feel great! Anna likes to sit with her feet pressed together in Butterfly pose.

Pigeon poses

These poses look easy, but they are deep stretches for your hips. With Double Pigeon, you can even stretch both hips at once. Remember to keep using the breath to help you hold these poses.

1 From Downward Dog pose, lift one leg high like Caroline is doing here.

2 Bend the knee as you bring down the leg, then reach it through towards the arms.

3 Rest the bent leg in a seated position. Palms press the mat. Lift the chest up high and lengthen the spine.

4 If you want to, try bending forwards to press your palms against the mat and rest.

Double pigeon

1 One heel stacks on top of your knee and the opposite knee is placed on top of your heel.

2 If you are comfortable, fold forwards and walk your fingers down the mat.

Dancer's Pose

Caroline and Christine balance in Dancer's Pose. Beginning with the feet together in Mountain pose, the girls raise their left arms. The right arm reaches back to take hold of the right ankle, gently lifting the back leg towards the sky.

Dancer's Pose is a great hip opener but a tough balancing act! It's OK to fall when you're trying poses.

"I like Dancer's Pose. It makes me feel like I am dancing."
Grant

Mary Kaye reminds the class to repeat each pose on the other side to keep the body in balance.

Frog pose

Caroline spreads her legs wide and squats in Frog pose. It's a great way to steady and calm the body. It's also fun to jump around in Frog pose!

Jumping Frogs!

Christine, Anna and Tara balance in Tree pose. One leg is bent with the foot placed inside the opposite leg. Holding the hands in prayer helps the girls stay centred.

All About Balance

The studio is quiet again for balance poses. The yogis have to concentrate on a gazing point and their breathing to hold these poses. Each pose shifts the body weight to balance on one spot – the left foot, right foot or bottom. You have to feel centred to stay straight and steady, so sometimes Mary Kaye asks the class to stand with their backs against the wall before they begin. This reminds the body what it feels like to stand up straight.

If you feel wobbly in Tree pose, place your foot farther down on the standing leg. This will give you better balance.

Boat pose

Caroline, Anna and Christine concentrate on holding Boat pose. Starting flat on their backs, the girls blow out their breath, or exhale, as they lift their arms and legs at the same time to form a human V. In Boat pose, you can feel your belly getting stronger.

Aeroplane

Tara lifts her body into Aeroplane pose. Keeping positive thoughts in mind can help make even the most challenging poses possible.

Yoga feet should be active. Spread the toes!

Drishti

The teacher will help you find your drishti, or gazing point, for each pose. You can look in front of you or find a spot on the floor, but do not watch your friend. If he wobbles, so will you!

Soar like an eagle

Mary Kaye tells the class to imagine standing on the edge of a mountain in Eagle pose. You are ready to fly!

Caroline wraps her right leg over her left leg. Then she wraps her left arm under her right arm.

The hands press together as Caroline squats low and steady. She gently tries to lift the elbows higher.

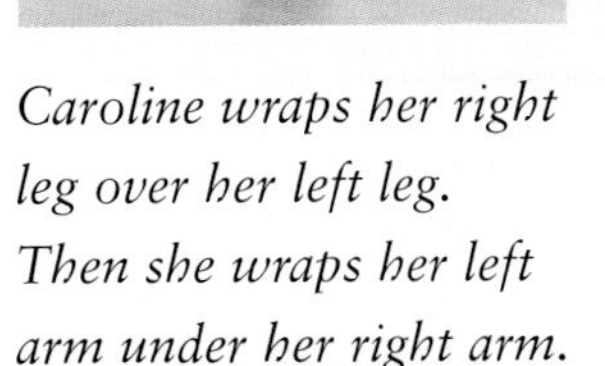

Power Poses

Power poses are a challenge for the body – but also a test of our mind's ability to stay calm and focused when things are hard. Caroline has practised for a long time to master these poses, but they have got easier for her as her belly and arms have become stronger, and she has learned to concentrate and use her breath.

Power poses require strength and calm. Each one is a different challenge, but don't give up – you can do it if you practise!

Crow pose

Crow pose is a test of balance, strength and trust in yourself. Remember to breathe and keep the gaze high so that your head feels light as a feather.

1 Caroline prepares for Crow in Seated Prayer pose. Her elbows gently press into her knees to open the hips.

2 Caroline places her hands on the mat and leans forwards. One knee comes up to rest high on the back of the arm.

Mermaid pose

Mermaid is an arm balance. It looks simple and beautiful, but it's hard to keep the feet and arms in position and keep steady.

Try straightening the legs and stacking the feet.

If you have trouble balancing, bring your knee to the floor for support.

Crow

If you're worried about falling, place a soft block on the mat in front of you. Crow is even more challenging if you lift your gaze high and straighten the arms. Remember: Your most important prop is confidence!

"I'm not afraid of falling anymore."
Caroline

3 Now the second knee comes high onto the back of the other arm. Try to lift the feet off the ground and balance the body.

Beginner Back Bends

Practising back-bend postures makes the spine more flexible. These poses open up the front of the body and awaken the senses. Back bends also help create energy in the body and stretch the shoulders, chest, thighs and belly. These poses can be fun and even a little bit silly – but they're a good way to take care of your spine and protect it from injury.

Cat pose

Cat/Cow poses

These poses help stretch out the back and chest. It's especially important with harder poses like back bends to do each pose together with its counterpose – that's why the Cat and Cow always come as a pair during class.

1 *In Cat pose, Anna begins on all fours and rounds out her back while inhaling deeply. The feet should lie flat on the mat.*

Table pose

Grant loves Table pose! In this pose, the legs, hands and arms have to work to support the body. The torso should be as flat as a table. Sometimes Grant walks like a crab in Table pose!

1 *Grant prepares for Table pose by sitting with raised, bent knees. The palms press into the mat, with fingertips facing towards the feet.*

2 *Grant lifts his hips and drops his head back. He closes his eyes and tries to stay still – but sometimes he can't help wiggling his toes and smiling!*

"I do Cat/Cow pose every night before bed."

Anna

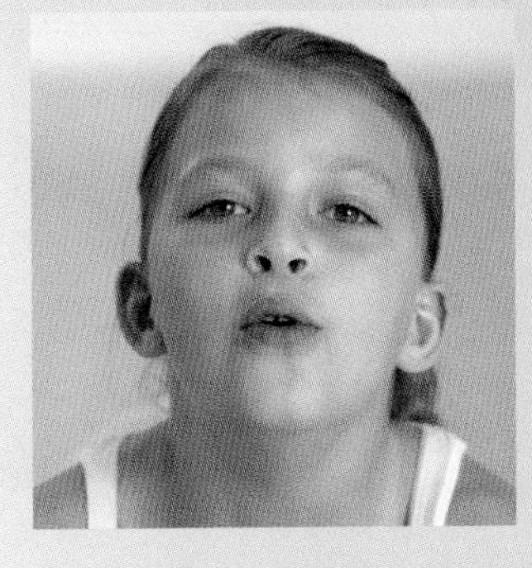

Anna gets into the spirit of Cow pose with a loud "Moooo!"

2 *In Cow pose, Anna lets her belly drop towards the floor while she exhales and lifts her chest.*

3 *Cat/Cow can also become a balance and stretch. Reach out one arm and the opposite foot. Pretend that something is pulling at each end.*

Bridge pose

Bridge pose opens your heart and shoulders and gives the back a great stretch. Tara likes this pose because it is restful and active at the same time.

1 *Tara lies flat on her back with arms flat on the mat along the sides of her body. The knees are bent and a few inches apart from each other.*

2 *The hips lift as Tara clasps her hands underneath her back and rests them on the mat. She slowly inches her shoulder blades closer together to raise her chest up.*

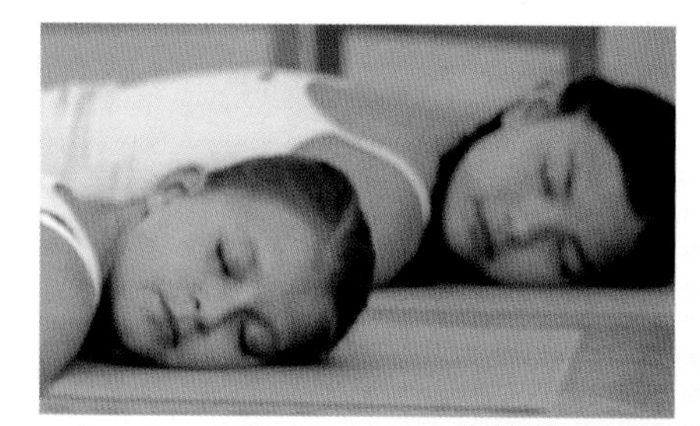

One of the class's favourite poses is resting 'cheek to mat' after working hard. It's nice to take a break after a deep back bend!

Advanced Back Bends

Mary Kaye says that flexibility helps open up areas in the body that hold stress and sadness – it can make us more confident and strong. Flexibility also helps you have good posture every day. All of these poses are designed to help you be more flexible. Some of them can be challenging, so try to hold them for just a couple of breaths at a time, then take a break and try again.

Bow pose

While lying on their bellies, Caroline, Anna and Christine bend their knees and reach back to hold their feet or ankles. As they breathe in, they lift their hearts to the sky. The girls breathe slowly in and out, lifting the head and feet higher with each breath.

King Cobra

1 *Caroline prepares in Cobra pose, breathing deeply. She lifts her head up, away from her shoulders.*

2 *Slowly bending at the knees, Caroline lifts her toes to the sky. The head tilts back toward the toes. Caroline can touch her toes to her head, but many of the students just reach as far as they can.*

"When I first started yoga, I couldn't do this pose. Now I can touch my toes to my head."

Caroline

Wheel pose

Wheel is a pose that requires strong arms. Your teacher should support your back while you are learning this pose.

1 *Prepare for Wheel by lying flat on the mat with bent knees. Tuck your feet close to your bottom.*

Fingertips are spread out flat against the mat.

2 *Pretend you have a string on your belly button that pulls your body up. Straighten your arms and let your head drop between them. Look straight ahead. Mary Kaye helps Caroline in Wheel by supporting her lower back.*

Upside Down

Upside-down poses are called inversions. Rag Doll, Gorilla and Shoulder Stand are inversions because they bring your heart above your head. Mary Kaye says that inversions are good for your brain and mental abilities. Plus, it's fun just to hang upside down!

Miles hangs in Rag Doll with his weight on the balls of his feet.

Try to stand on your hands to massage your wrists.

Gorilla pose

As you hang your head heavy in Rag Doll, let your hands drop to the floor. Now place your palms under your feet. Picture how a gorilla walks in the rainforest. Mary Kaye makes gorilla noises in this pose!

Shoulder Stand

Shoulder Stand, also known as Candle pose, is an inversion that is helpful for circulation. Shoulder Stands help circulate fresh blood to your brain and send energy to the toes. They are also very calming, so Mary Kaye likes to do them towards the end of class.

1 *Christine prepares for Shoulder Stand by lying flat on her back with her knees bent towards the ceiling.*

Make sure your weight rests on your arms and shoulders, not your neck.

2 The knees lift up to hover over Christine's forehead. She walks her hands up her back as she lifts up to rest on her elbows.

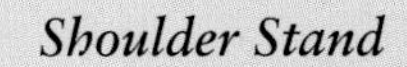

Shoulder Stand

3 Now the toes raise straight up while the shoulders and hands support the back. Christine presses her chin to her chest and relaxes the neck.

Plough pose

4 After holding Shoulder Stand, Christine drops her feet all the way to the mat to relax in Plough pose. It's OK if your feet do not touch the mat. Just continue to support your back.

Energy Moves Me

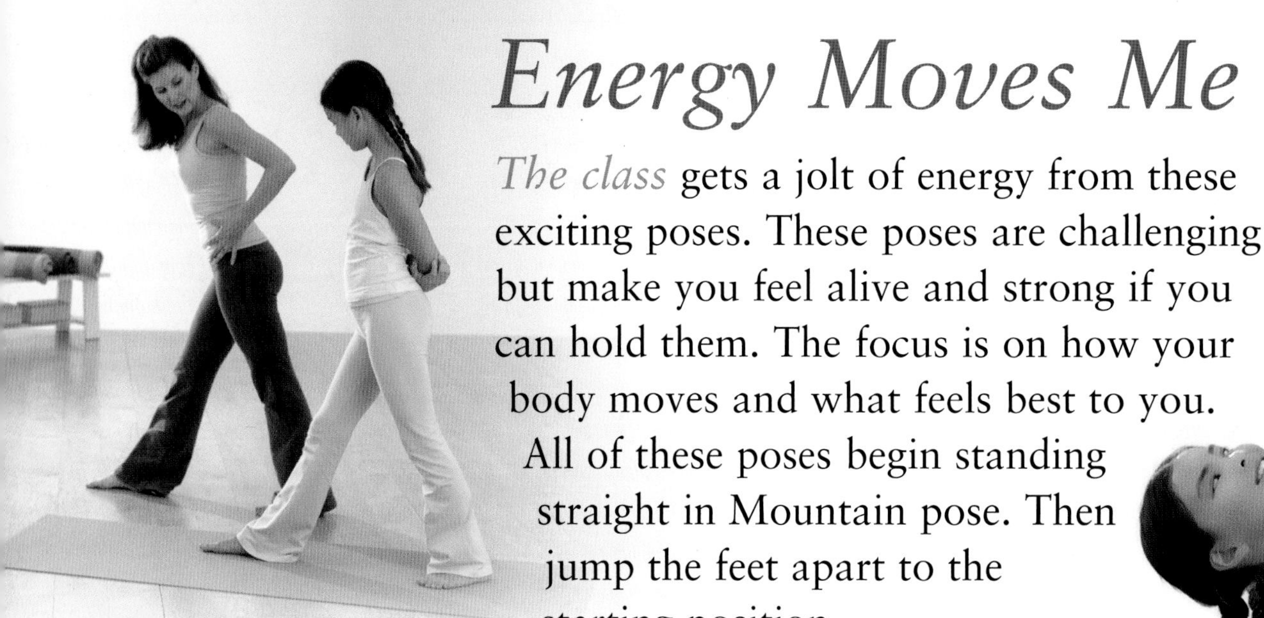

The class gets a jolt of energy from these exciting poses. These poses are challenging but make you feel alive and strong if you can hold them. The focus is on how your body moves and what feels best to you. All of these poses begin standing straight in Mountain pose. Then jump the feet apart to the starting position.

Mary Kaye helps Christine remember to face the hips forwards in Warrior One.

Use a block in Triangle pose to help you balance.

Warrior poses

Warrior poses move energy through the fingertips and the legs. Anna loves the way they make her feel powerful and graceful.

Warrior One

In Warrior One, the front knee is bent, and the torso faces forwards. Anna presses the back foot into the mat.

Warrior Two

In Warrior Two, the hips turn to the side and the arms stretch out. The back leg stays straight and strong as Anna bends deep into the pose.

Steeple Grip

Anna brings the hands together in Steeple Grip and shifts her weight forwards.

Warrior Three

The front leg straightens as Anna lifts the back leg and brings the chest parallel to the ground. The body should stay in a straight line – it's easier with someone to help!

Triangle pose

This pose imitates the straight lines of a triangle. But don't worry about making your pose look exactly like one – it's all about having fun and learning how to breathe while holding the pose. Look up to the sky, open your heart and feel the energy stretching from fingertip to fingertip and down your legs.

You can also try this pose with hands behind the back in Reverse Prayer.

Side Stretch

From Warrior pose, walk the back foot in slightly and hold opposite elbows. Side Stretch is good for loosening the leg muscles and lengthening the spine.

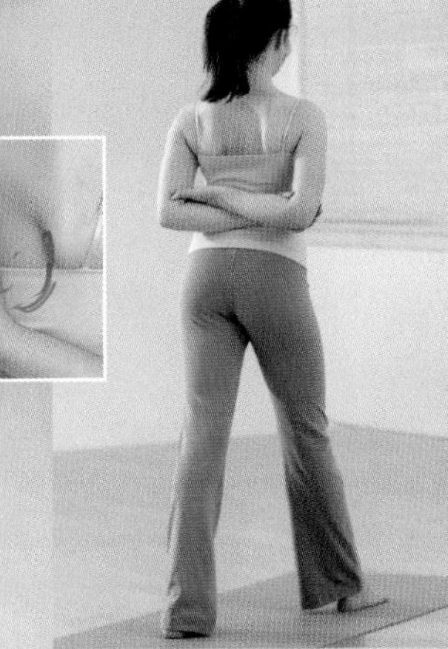

1 *Tara steps the legs apart with both feet facing forwards. Arms are folded behind the back.*

2 *She folds forwards while lifting the heart, bringing the head towards the knee. Her gaze is straight ahead.*

3 *The forehead reaches towards the knee. Remember to keep the back straight!*

In this Seated Twist, Caroline uses all the parts of the body – even the gaze of the eyes – to help her twist in the same direction. Even in a twist, it's important to sit up tall.

Twist and Split

Twists and splits create a side stretch that helps keep the muscles and organs in your belly healthy, and can improve balance. Like all yoga poses, they can also help settle the mind. Your twists and splits will change with practice, so don't worry if you can't stretch very wide or deep in the beginning. Use your breath to loosen the muscles a little more each time, and enjoy the stretch.

Reclining twist

Lie on your back with legs extended and arms stretched out. Breathe out and bend your right knee over your left leg. Now look to your right and gently use your left arm to press your knee down towards the floor.

Straddle Split

This sequence is a good hip stretch. It also helps your body get comfortable with splits. The poses don't have to be very low or wide – it's all about finding the right place for your body.

1 *Tara prepares for Straddle Split by placing her hands on her hips and jumping her legs open.*

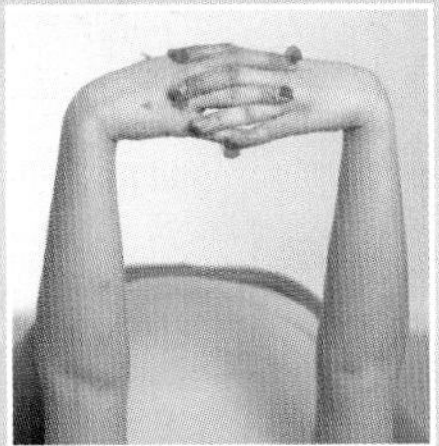

Clasp the hands firmly.

2 *Tara interlaces her fingers behind her back. Then she folds forwards and lets her hands fall over her head towards the floor. The outer sides of her feet press into the mat.*

3 *In Straddle position, the hands reach forwards to the ground. One hand then reaches up as the gaze follows it. Then the raised hand slowly comes down as the other reaches up.*

4 *Finally, Tara straddles her legs and takes slow, deep breaths as she slides towards the floor a little at a time. Do not force yourself to touch the floor.*

"Yoga helps at all sports because it improves your balance."

Tara

Caroline and Anna sit in Lotus pose with palms pressed together. Mary Kaye says that the power of touch can be healing.

Partner Yoga

Caroline and Anna love partner poses because they get to work as a team. It feels good to support each other and talk and laugh together. Partner yoga is also a reminder of how important it is to give and ask for help with poses when you need it. Remember to say thank you for the help you receive!

London Bridge

This London Bridge is strong! The partners face each other and touch toes. Holding hands, they stretch the legs to the sky.

Don't forget to laugh – partner yoga is about being supportive and having fun, no matter how well you can hold a pose!

Bound Lotus

Bound Lotus pose is a way to warm up with a friend. The partners support each other as they stretch their bodies.

The arms link together.

Each girl takes a turn leaning back while her partner supports her. This movement should be fun – but remember to treat your body gently as you stretch.

Fun and Games

In yoga class, we always make time for games! There are lots of ways to have fun with yoga. You can balance the blocks on your head or act out an imaginary story using the animal poses. Today, the class is trying a Bundle Roll. There are no losers in this game – in yoga, everybody wins!

Shark and Bundle Roll

In Bundle Roll, the children lie side by side on the floor and then roll across the floor together. Mary Kaye picks one of the youngest yogis to act like a fierce shark. When the children start rolling, their movement makes the shark start to swim!

Practise Shark

1 Grant lies on his belly in Shark pose. His hands are clasped in Steeple Grip. Then he lifts his heart and legs up high at the same time.

2 Now quickly – swim away from the shark! Grant moves his arms and legs to swim to safety.

Practise Roll

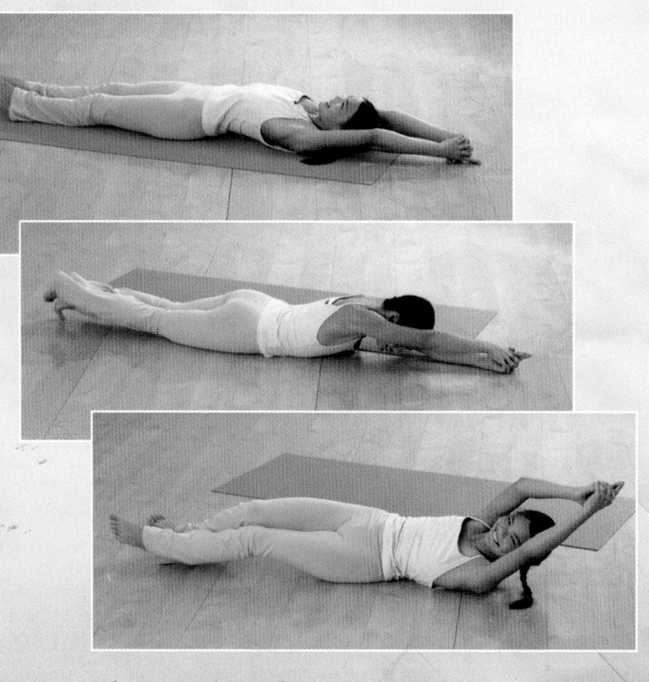

Christine shows how to practise the Bundle Roll. She starts on her mat with her body straight and her hands pressed together in Steeple Grip. Then she rolls!

1 The children lie on the floor with their shoulders together to prepare for Bundle Roll. Then Mary Kaye picks up Grant in Shark pose.

2 Mary Kaye places the shark on top of the 'bundles' and tells them to roll on the count of three.

Everybody ready?

One, two, three – roll!

"I love to be the shark!"

Grant

Here comes the shark!

Restful Poses

Just breathe. At the end of class, the children wind down by moving slowly and keeping a steady breath. They have worked hard and have earned a break. Mary Kaye guides the class through some poses that relax the body. Everyone tries to keep their minds clear of negative thoughts and concentrate on the breath. This is the time to be happy and just be.

Soothing stretches

These stretches help the body cool down at the end of class. Try not to worry about what you look like in the poses – just enjoy how they feel to your legs and back.

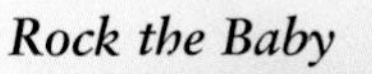

Rock the Baby

Anna and Caroline lie on their backs in Dead Bug pose. They hold each foot by the inner arch and press their knees towards the ground.

Dead Bug pose

Tara relaxes her legs with a soothing stretch. This pose is called Rock the Baby because the leg is gently cradled while hugged close to the chest.

Happy Baby pose

Caroline extends her legs to change Dead Bug into Happy Baby pose.

Child's pose

This peaceful pose is the perfect way to rest your body at the end of class or after a difficult pose.

"I feel so relaxed and peaceful after yoga class."
Caroline

Take water breaks during class to keep your body hydrated.

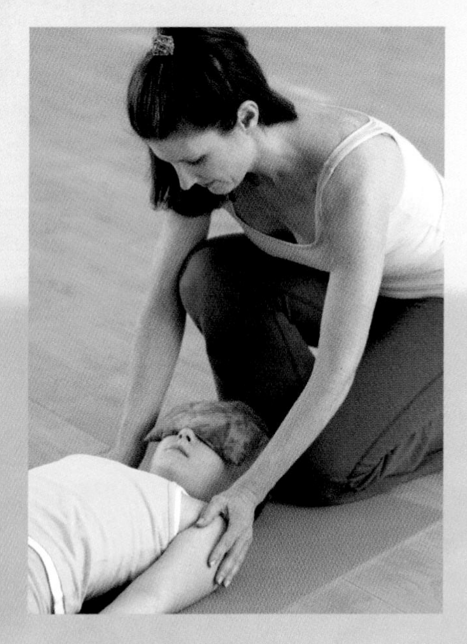

Mary Kaye presses gently on Caroline's shoulders to help her release tension.

Savasana

This is one of the best parts of class – but it can also be the most challenging. 'Savasana' is the Sanskrit word for 'Corpse pose'. Try to lie completely still and allow the tension to leave your body. Close your eyes and calm your mind. Release all the muscles in your face, relax your jaw, unclench your teeth, soften your tongue. The entire body melts into the mat. Rest and be still – this is the reward for all your hard work during class.

Corpse pose

In Corpse pose, everybody lies still on their mats. Some people use blocks or blankets under their back or knees. You can also cover your body with a blanket to stay toasty warm. Try to relax your body and empty your mind of all thoughts in this pose. Pretend you are a large sandbag with a tiny hole, and all your sand is slowly pouring out onto your mat.

An eye pillow can help you block out distractions. Gentle music and soothing scents like lavender or jasmine can also help you relax.

Sitting up

When it's time to get up, Mary Kaye guides the class to sit up inch by inch, slowly waking their minds and bodies. Coming out of Savasana is a time to rest and enjoy silence, so take it slowly.

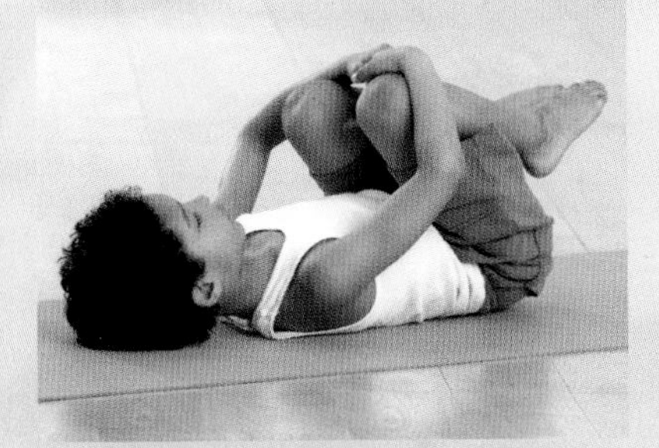

1 *Stretch your arms around your legs and hug your knees to your chest.*

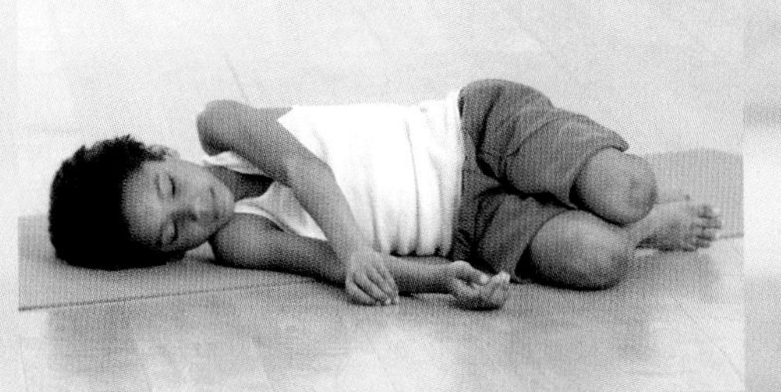

2 *Keep your eyes closed and roll over to your right side, letting your arms and legs fall onto the floor.*

3 *Now roll up to sit. Keep your eyes closed until you feel ready to open them. You can put your hands on your knees and meditate in this position.*

"I pretend my thoughts are clouds and watch them float away."
Miles

Namaste

At the end of class, Mary Kaye and the children chant "Om". This chant is the sound of the world at peace. Then Mary Kaye bows her head with her hands raised in prayer position and says "Namaste". Namaste means "may the light in me, greet the light in you". This is the class's way of saying farewell.

Namaste!

Anna *Caroline* *Tara*

Miles

Christine

Grant

Glossary

A

Asana – pose which really means "take a comfortable seat".

B

Balance – holding the body so that both sides are equal.

C

Chant – a simple song that can be sung to help your mind and body relax.

D

Drishti – a gazing point for a pose.

F

Flexibility – the ability to bend your body in many different ways.

I

Inversion – an upside down pose.

M

Meditation – taking quiet time to rest your mind and senses.

N

Namaste – (nah-mah-STAY) a Hindu greeting meaning "may the light in me, greet the light in you".

O

Om – a vibrational sound of the world at peace. It contains the letter sounds A, U and M.

P

Pose – a position that the body takes to stretch, balance or rest.

S

Sanskrit – a very old Indian language. In yoga, every pose has a Sanskrit name.

Savasana – corpse pose: *sava* means 'corpse' in Sanskrit, and this pose is the first step in the practice of meditation.

Steeple Grip – a hand position that looks like the shape of a church steeple. The fingers are interlaced with the index fingers extended.

Stretch – a type of exercise that helps to loosen up your muscles.

U

Ujjayi – means 'victorious breath' and is breathing that sounds like an ocean.

V

Vinyasa – poses linked by the breath; Sun Salutation is a vinyasa.

Y

Yoga Toe Lock – a way to grip the foot by hooking two fingers around the big toe.

Yogi – a student of yoga.

Index

Acknowledgements

Dorling Kindersley would like to thank the following for their help in the preparation and production of this book:

Tyler, Ashton and Grant Chryssicas, Anna Pops, Christine Tsai and Myles Holt for their cooperation and amazing strength; Angela Coppola and Donna Mancini at Coppola Studios, Ted Chryssicas for all his help, and of course the indefatigable Mary Kaye.

From the author: Special thanks to my family, friends, yoga teachers and the staff at DK, especially Beth Hester, my talented editor with the kind soul, who have encouraged me and helped me develop my interest in yoga to make this book possible. Thanks also to the little yogis who inspire me every day, and our back up yoga models, Sophie Mussafer, Patrick Milmoe and Charlie Gordon. This book is my way of bringing the world of yoga to the younger generation who can really benefit from it.

Check out www.buddhafulkids.com to learn more about Mary Kaye's classes and kids' yoga.